COMMANDING ABUNDANCE

The thoughts of the diligent tend only to plenty
Proverb 21:5

BY

FRANKLIN N ABAZIE

COMMANDING ABUNDANCE
The thoughts of the diligent tend only to plenty

Copyright © 2009 by Franklin N Abazie

All rights reserved. This book or any portion thereof may not be reproduced or used in any manner whatsoever without the express written permission of the publisher, except for the use of brief quotations in a book review. All Bible quotes are from King James Version and others as noted.

Published by F N Abazie Publishing House, marketed and Sold by F N Abazie Bookshop also called Empowerment Bookstore

Psalm 26:7 "that I may publish with a voice of thanksgiving and tell of all thy wondrous works"
To order additional copies, wholesale or bookings:
Write or call

Miracle of God Ministries

33 Schley Street; Newark, NJ 07112

Church Office: (973) 372-7518

www.fnabaziehealingministries.org
Email: pastorfranknto@yahoo.com

TABLE OF CONTENTS

Acknowledgement v
The Mandate of the Commission viii
Chapter 1. Have Dominion Over All 1
Chapter 2. Replenish The Earth And Subdue It 27
Chapter 3. Be Fruitful And Multiply. 31
Chapter 4. Abundance Above Measures 43
Chapter 5. Healing Restoration 49
Chapter 6. Prayer Points For Abundance 55
Prayer of Salvation 59
About the Author 65

ACKNOWLEDGEMENT

I would like to first thank God for His infinite grace and mercy that has allowed me to finally write and publish this book. I would also like to acknowledge Rev Dr. David Jefferson Sr., whom the Holy Ghost used as a vessel to deliver the classical great salvation message that touched my life and converted me into a born again Christian on March 28th 1999.

Despite the obstacles and challenges I faced writing this book. The Holy Spirit allowed me to witness unprecedented challenges and hindrances putting this book together, so that I could be properly trained, matured, endowed with deed insight on how to properly addressed, sanction and position the enemy. More also it was a test of my writing and analytical thinking skill to prepare me for my subsequent new books. I want to thank my lovely wife and my beloved three children for all their support.

This book will not be complete without me expressing my gratitude to my oldest brother Elder Festus N Abazie. Elder Festus was the human tool and divine machinery which the Lord used immensely to transform my live in 1997. Sir Festus I love you with all my heart and remain ever thankful to God and to you for all your support.

Commanding Abundance

THE MANDATE OF THE COMMISSION

"THE MOMENT IS DUE TO IMPACT YOUR WORLD THROUGH THE REVIVAL OF THE HEALING & MIRACLE MINISTRY OF JESUS CHRIST OF NAZARETH

I AM SENDING YOU TO RESTORE HEALTH UNTO THEE AND I WILL HEAL THEE OF THY WOUNDS. SAID THE LORD OF HOST"

Franklin N Abazie

ARMS OF THE COMMISSION

1. F N Abazie Ministries: Miracle of God Healing Church (Miracle Chapel Intl)

2. F N Abazie TV Ministries: Global Television Ministry Outreach

3. F N Abazie Radio Ministries: Radio Broadcasting Outreach

4. F N Abazie Publishing House: Book Publication

5. F N Abazie Bible School: also called Word of Healing Bible School (W.O.H.B.S)

6. F N Abazie Evangelistic Ass: Miracle of God Ministries: Global Crusade

7. Empowerment Bookstore: Book distribution

8. F N Abazie Helping Hands: Meeting the help of the needy world wide

9. F N Abazie Disaster Recovery Mission: Global Disaster Recovery

10. F N Abazie Prison Ministry: Prison Ministry for all convicts "Second chance

Some of our ministry arms are waiting the appointed time to commence.

CHAPTER 1

HAVE DOMINION OVER ALL

Genesis 1:28.... Have dominion over the fish of the sea, and over the fowl of the air, and over every living thing that moveth upon the earth

The above scripture is God's dominion mandate that has been conferred and commissioned unto man here on earth. It is a scriptural commandment for you and I to have dominion over every living thing. Furthermore, it is scripturally ordained for us to not only have dominion, but more also to subdue the earth.

Franklin N Abazie

How do I have dominion one may ask?

Job 22:21-25

Acquaint now thyself with him, and be at peace: thereby good shall come unto thee. Receive, I pray thee, the law from his mouth, and lay up his words in thine heart.

If thou return to the Almighty, thou shalt be built up, thou shalt put away iniquity far from thy tabernacles. Then shalt thou lay up gold as dust, and the gold of Ophir as the stones of the brooks. Yea, the Almighty shall be thy defence, and thou shalt have plenty of silver.

Based on the preceding scripture, to command dominion, first you must desire the peace of God that surpasses all understanding. Next you must lay up His words in your heart.

Lastly, it is a commandment; you must put away iniquity far from your life. HENCE YOU WILL BE BUIT UP AND YOU SHALL COMMAND DOMINION.

Wisdom demands that we understand the know-how, techniques and relevant approach to command dominion in life. "One man said life is in phase and men are in seizes"

Psalms 23:5

Thou preparest a table before me in the presence of mine enemies.

We are admonished by the above scripture to command dominion in the presence of our enemies. It is of necessity for you to understand that there is a vital and crucial battle before any conferment. No champion emerges without defeating another champion. However, many people claim to command dominion by intellectual and secular knowledge. This is not true in the Spiritual realm and in the kingdom of God. In the realms of the Spirit it takes a fight for every champion to emerge. 1tim6:12 Fight the good fight of faith. lay hold on eternal life, whereunto thou art also called. And hast professed a good profession before many witnesses.Psalms 119:98 Thou through thy commandments hast made me wiser than mine enemies: for they are ever with me.

What type of abundance and fight are we talking about?

Life is full of warfare's. In this life you will be opposed with challenges, you will witness obstacles and difficulties. Otherwise stated the devil has long vowed to attack you, therefore unless you make up your mind to put up a fight against the adversary, you are heading for defeat. In this physical world we live in today, there are a lot of abundance of the things you desire all over the earth today.

What is abundance?

The American heritage dictionary defines abundance as a great or plenteous amount; fullness to overflowing; affluence; wealth. It is in God's will, and in His plan for man, to live a life of fullness and to overflow; to live a life of affluence and wealth. Nevertheless, Satan has always been an opposition and a threat to the life of man.

It is interesting to remind you yet again that it has always been the will of God for you and I to command abundance because He has given us dominion over every living thing. Despite what Satan may try to do, the Almighty God established man to have dominion over all. Regrettably, multitudes of believers have forgotten their dominion mandate. Many have become beggars and slaves even at the mercy of fellow Christians. Multitudes are dying of sickness and disease because they have forgotten, or do not know about, their dominion heritage. The plague of poverty has taken missions of Christians captive, hence our God given dominion mandate has been forgotten.

Every faithful small step you take in the area God has called is a righteous step toward your dominion in that area. Every small sincere beginning is a step that will lead you to the top of the world. Microsoft was not built in one day. Job8:7 Though thy beginning was small, yet thy latter end should greatly increase. If the truth be told, there is no curse upon your life. You were not created and destined to be poor in life. For there is no difference between the Jew and the Greek; for the same lord over all is rich unto all that call upon him. Romans10:12

Beloved in Christ, may I remind you that God owns the cattle's upon the thousand rams. May I address to you that the Gold and the silver belongs unto our God (See Haggai2:6-8, Psalms 24:1, Psalms 50:12, Romans 10:12).

For there is no difference between the Jew and the Greek; for the same lord over all is rich unto all that call upon him. Romans10:12

It has always been in God's agenda for us to command abundance. (Psalms 35:27). Furthermore, it has always been the will of God for His children to live and command a life of abundance (3 John 1:2). Regrettably, many Christians have been robbed of their riches, honor, inheritance and blessings. You and I have been robbed of the exceedingly precious promise, which was supposed to convert us as partakers of His divine nature.

Zig Ziglar once said, "Just any dummy can succeed, if he cares to learn how to succeed."

What does it mean to have dominion over all?

To have dominion means to be in command of all things. This I mean to possess all that wealth and riches offers. Look at **Obadiah** 1:17 as it says, "***And the house of Jacob shall possess their possessions*** To have dominion means to in-charge and to take the lead in life. It also means to have power and authority necessary to establish, declare and legislate, delegate; to regulate, make laws, rules, regulations and legislation; To have dominion in life also means to execute, to issue ordinances and be able to be in command of your life, other and be in command of your territory, region and nation. Every Christian must have dominion over all, otherwise, how do you differentiate between a believer and an unbeliever? How do you tell the difference between someone that serves God and the one that doesn't serve Him? (See Malachi 3:18)

Furthermore, to have dominion means to be in command of your spiritual territory. Satan has harassed and deceived the people of God long enough. It is time for every believer to rise up in faith and begin to take command and exercise dominion over every living thing in their life, domain and jurisdiction. It is time to return integrity and dignity to the house of God. In addition, it is time for the prosperity of the saints of God to be released.

COMMANDING DOMINION PRAYER POINTS

1. O Lord of heaven, have mercy upon my life.

2. Father of light, visit my life with divine speed.

3. Omnipotent Father of grace, restore my mind.

4. Holy Ghost fire, burn up all the chaff of the enemy in my life.

5. Blood of Jesus, terminate the assignment of the devil over my life.

6. Spirit of God, saturate my being, in the name of Jesus.

7. All owners of evil loads must carry their load over my life this time, in the name of Jesus

8. Hand of God, I am ready to be catapulted into my abundance, in the name of Jesus.

9. Angels of prosperity, locate me, in the name of Jesus.

10. Power to prosper, hit me and drive me like a wave, in the name of Jesus.

Commanding Abundance

PRAYER POINTS TO MOVE FORWARD IN LIFE

1. Any power hiding the keys of my elevation, receive double failure, in Jesus' name.

2. Every stronghold of the power of familiar spirits in my destiny, die, in the name of Jesus.

3. Evil gossipers assigned against my prosperity, die, in the name of Jesus.

4. Every spiritual bat programmed against my divine assignment, die now, in the name of Jesus.

5. Every spiritual vulture programmed against my life, die now, in Jesus' name.

6. Every spiritual dog programmed against my divine future, die now, in the name of Jesus.

7. I crush every satanic lion from rising against my progress, in the name of Jesus.

8. O Lord, I refuse to live under any satanic cloud, in the name of Jesus.

9. O Lord, sweep oppressors with the broom of destruction.

10. Let every evil power increasing against me fall down and die, in the name of Jesus.

Commanding Abundance

PRAYER POINT TO DISMANTLE FAILURE IN LIFE

1. I paralyze all aggression addressed to my star, in the name of Jesus.

2. Lord, bring honey out of the rock for me this month.

3. Lord, open up all the good doors of my life that household wickedness has shut.

4. Let all anti-breakthrough designs against my life be shattered to irreparable pieces, in the name of Jesus.

5. I paralyze all satanic antagonism against my destiny from the womb, in Jesus' name

6. I trample upon every enemy of my advancement and I unseat evil powers sitting on my promotions, in Jesus' name.

7. O Lord, enlarge my coast beyond my wildest dreams, in the name of Jesus.

8. I claim back all my goods presently residing in the wrong hands, in the name of Jesus.

9. O Lord, plant good things that will advance my cause into my life.

10. Every imprisoned and buried potential, come forth now, in the name of Jesus.

ANOINTING TO PROSPER PRAYERS POINTS

1. I break the curse of automatic failure working in any department of my life, in the name of Jesus.

2. Let the anointing to excel and prosper fall mightily upon every department of my life, in Jesus' name.

3. Let every anti-progress altar fashioned against me be destroyed with the fire of God, in Jesus' name.

4. I withdraw my benefits from the hands of the oppressors, in the name of Jesus.

5. Let every power chasing blessings away from me be paralyzed, in the name of

Jesus.

6. Let the enemy begin to vomit every good thing they have eaten up in my life, in the name of Jesus.

7. O Lord, give me power to overcome every obstacle to my breakthroughs.

8. I break all curses of leaking blessings, in the name of Jesus.

9. I clear my goods from the warehouse of the strongman, in the name of Jesus.

Commanding Abundance

PRAYER POINT TO GO FORWARD IN LIFE

1. Let all the adversaries of my breakthroughs be put to shame, in the name of Jesus.

2. I claim the power to overcome and to excel amongst all competitors, in Jesus' name.

3. Let any decision by any panel be favorable unto me, in the name of Jesus.

4. Every negative word and pronouncement against my success be completely nullified, in Jesus' name.

5. I bind every spirit manipulating my benefactors against me, in the name of Jesus.

6. I remove my name from the book of seers of goodness without appropriation, in the name of Jesus.

7. Let the cloud blocking the sunlight of my glory and breakthrough be dispersed, in the name of Jesus.

8. Lord, let wonderful changes begin to be my lot from this week.

9. I reject every spirit of the tail in all areas of my life, in the name of Jesus.

10. Oh Lord, bring me into favor with all those that will decide on my advancement.

11. Oh Lord, cause a divine substitution to happen if this is what will move me ahead.

Commanding Abundance

12. I reject the spirit of the tail and I claim the spirit of the head, in the name of Jesus.

13. Oh Lord, transfer, remove or change all human agents that are bent on stopping my advancement.

14. All demonic chains preventing my advancement, be broken, in the name of Jesus.

Franklin N Abazie

HOW DO I IMPLEMENT THE STRATEGY TO HAVE DOMINION OVER MY LIFE?

Every greatness in life must start from the heart. The bible says with the heart man believeth unto righteousness and with the mouth confession is made unto salvation. If you believe you can be great in life, and do what attracts greatness in life; you will eventually be great in life. In my own view poverty and wealth is a decision of the heart. The bible says as a man thinketh in his heart so is he. Believe me as I say it here, Satan has lost every atom of power. Satan lost the battle when Jesus hung on the cross on Calvary.

Secondly, you must understand the strength of the enemy.

Commanding Abundance

2 Corinthians 4:4

"In whom the God of this world hath blinded the minds of them which believed not, lest the light of the glorious gospel of Christ, who is the image of God, should shine unto them."

Satan has an hour and the power of darkness (See Luke 22:53). You have been oppressed and frustrated in your life because of the powers of darkness. Maybe you feel passive concerning your right to command your abundance. Let me point something out to you: God has given you the ability to think well and reflect. If you can think well with your mind, your hands will be very productive (See II Thessalonians 3:10).

Isaiah 60:2

"For behold, the darkness shall cover the

earth, and gross darkness the people: but the lord shall rise upon thee and his glory shall be seen upon thee. "

I know that your biggest challenge is finances (money). Permit me to say this to you: you start small to grow big; "it is only in digging the grave; that digging starts at the top".

You cannot command abundance without having dominion over all (superior power). It was not until David killed Goliath, who was the champion of the Philistines that he was made fit for the palace. Perhaps you are not a preacher or an author, but there is a gift from God inside of you. Proverbs 18:16 says, "Your gift will bring you before great men." Settle it in your heart, this very day that if you will be willing in life; that God will make a way for you in life., because II Corinthians

Commanding Abundance

9:8 says, "And God is able to make all grace abound towards you; that ye always having all sufficiency in all things may about to every good work."   Despite any work of darkness to hinder your life, if you accept what God has placed in you, according to His word, you will stand before great men and He will give you the grace to perform every good work associated with the call of God upon your life.

There are a few scriptures that lead directly to abundance. Read and meditate on them. Allow them and their meaning to soak into your spirit. Apply what you learn from them.

Psalm 90:16-17

"let thy work appear unto their children. And let the beauty of the lord our God be upon us and establish thou the work of our hands upon us yea; the work of our hands establish thou it."

Psalm 27:1

"the Lord is my light and my salvation; whom shall I fear? The lord is the strength of my life; of whom shall I be afraid."

Psalm 35:27 let them shout for joy and be glad that favour my righteous cause; yea let them say continually, let the lord be magnified, which hath pleasure in the prosperity of his servant.

3 John 1:2

Beloved, wish above all things that thou mayest prosper and be in health, even as thy soul prospereth.

CHAPTER 2

REPLENISH THE EARTH AND SUBDUE IT

...... Replenish the earth, and subdue it: and have dominion over the fish of the sea, and over the fowl of the air, and over every living thing that moveth upon the earth. Genesis 1:28

Without any contradiction, man was created to enjoy the pleasures of life from fullness to overflow. The first man, Adam, had the pleasure of naming each animal. However, Adam and Eve, in the midst of divine abundance created by God, were evicted from the Garden of Eden as a result of sin.

Henceforth, man found himself in the midst of lack.

Today, man despite all his search and quest for power and dominion is still a prey at the mercy of the devil. (for those who lack the word of God) man has gone from the moon to under the sea with the aim to search for power and to dominate and subdue that power. In man's carnal pursuit of life's luxuries, every mineral resource from potassium to coal, and gold to ivory has been put to good and effective use.

Ecclesiastes 10:15

"the labor of the foolish wearieth every one of them because he knoweth not how to go to the city."

Although God has promised and covenanted with us but If you do not possess the know-how, the strategy and techniques to command abundance, you will remain in penury. In this life we become great by obeying instructions from the Lord. Instructions from God are wisdom guidelines. Every one committed to following Gods genuine instruction is a candidate heading to the top.

What do you do for a living?

I know you have been an employee of that organization for a long time, but have you ever considered becoming an employer of labor? Have you ever considered starting your own business? The Bible says that with God all things are possible (See Mark 10:27, Luke 1:37). Perhaps you do not have a job right now, however, remain hopeful because not long from now, you will locate a job!

There may be a need for you to go back to school. Whatever the case may be, no matter your current status, desire a change and work towards it. God will meet you with abundance to accomplish it. The desired change for your life will come. One man said that the largest room in the world is the room for improvement. If truly you desire abundance in life, you will be attracted to the things that guarantees abundance in life.

CHAPTER 3

BE FRUITFUL AND MULTIPLY

By virtue of the capacity of human brain, we are wired and designed to think innovative and creative thoughts. We can imagine mystical things and create it. To be fruitful and to multiply means to have a brain child. Someone someday started Google the internet giant company, someone someday started Facebook. So many people have ignored the scriptural interpretation of the above scripture "Be fruitful and multiply." There are some relevant steps in life that will guarantee to be , fruitful and to multiply. I have outlined some relevant genuine steps that will guarantee fruitfulness and multiplication in this race of life. Therefore let us briefly examine some of those crucial steps:

1). **Divine Ideas:** Divine ideas are very creative. Every divine idea genuinely nurtured has the potential to command abundance, plenty of wealth and make you command affluence in your life. It was a divine idea that brought Jacob more wages than what Laban was to pay him (See Genesis 30:25-43). Divine ideas will grant you fame, respect, power and prestige above all. Divine ideas are given by God to whom He pleases (See James 1:17). Take a minute to pray and ask God to give you your own divine idea that will enable you to make a difference in society and have a global impact. Someday two young boys started a technology transportation company called UBER. This internet transportation giant are taking over transportation business all over the continental USA. Divine ideas is the key success in life. Pulse and pray for God to release your own innovative and creative idea to gain wealth and command abundance in the Name of Jesus. Amen

2).**Wisdom:** Every wisdom from above comes from the wisest God. God gives wisdom freely to everyone. Although wisdom is the custodian of wealth, there are other necessary components that must be active for anyone to command abundance. King Solomon said, in Proverbs 13:11, "wealth gotten by vanity shall diminish, but he that gathereth by labor shall increase." It is important to mention the instructions for labor in Proverbs 23:4: "labor not to be rich, cease from thine own wisdom."

Therefore, let us briefly examine another necessary component for commanding abundance: Ecclesiastes 8:1 says, "who is as the wise man? And who knoweth the interpretation of a thing? A man's wisdom maketh his face to shine, and the boldness of his face shall be changed." Simply defined, wisdom is profitable to direct. You and I cannot command abundance without the wisdom of God.

In my own definition wisdom is the Supernatural hand of God in the life of a man. Our ministry was not taking off and growing as I would desire it to grow, so I discovered I needed the wisdom of God in my ministry so I began seeking God and asking for wisdom to do His will in my ministry calling.

Few months later the Holy Spirit began to manifest upon my life and ministry. Do not seek for God where God does not want you to be. For example; So many people play the state lottery with an ambition to win, not with a vision from God. Now, playing the lottery is gambling in the first place, and the bible is against gambling. Secondly so many people play to win it, but remember the lottery is some one's divine idea designed to make money.

3). **Learning:** In this life no man is above learning something new from somewhere. No one can master any trade without learning. Learning is the foundation for mastering a skills. No one can call themselves an expert in any discipline without learning. Learning means apprenticeship. Bishop Abioye once said, "Yesterday you yearned, today you learned, tomorrow you will earn." Let me rephrase it this way: after learning you will earn money to command abundance in your life. In I Timothy 4:13 it says, "Till I come, give attendance to reading, to exhortation, to doctrine." Every great man is a man of continuous learning. If you are a committed learner, you are destined to become a great leader in life.

4). **Knowledge:** Simply defined, knowledge means information. No one can command abundance without information. Proverbs 11:9 says, "through knowledge shall the just be delivered." Knowledge grants you information; information plus applied revelation will bring the desired revolution (commanding abundance).

5). **Understanding:** Proverbs 13:15 says, "A good understanding giveth favor." You will remain in confusion until understanding comes. It is vital to understand your steps and what to do when it is time to command abundance in your life (See Psalms 119:99-100).

6). **Reasoning:** Isaiah 1:18 says, "come now, and let us reason together; saith the Lord." The prodigal son reasoned himself out of bondage and returned to his father.

Luke 15:17-18

"And when he came to himself, he said how many hired servant of my fathers have bread enough and to spare, and I perish with hunger. I will arise and go to my father, and will say unto him father, I have sinned against heaven, and before thee."

One great study reveals that only about five percent of the human populace thinks; fifteen percent think they are thinking, while the other eighty percent would rather die than think. You are fearfully and wonderfully made only if you can reason and think appropriately.

7). **Meditation:** Psalms 119:99: "I have more understanding than all my teachers for thy testimonies are my meditation." You cannot command abundance if you cannot reflect and meditate on the fact that it is even possible to command abundance.

8). Vision: For every one that desires to command abundance, there must be a vision. Vision will drive any destiny into motion. It is Vision that gives birth to purpose. There is one thing that you can be known for the rest of your life. Vision will bring discipline and focus. It will enable you to concentrate on one thing in your life. Discover Gods Vision

Commanding Abundance

for your life and enjoy divine rest in Gods agenda. Proverbs 29:18

"Without a vision the people perish but he that keepeth the law happy is he."

Every genuine vision from God will command abundance. I urge you to locate God's divine vision for your life today and begin to command your spiritual, material and financial abundance, in the name of Jesus, Amen.

God's fruitful and multiplication agenda for mankind was out of His love for man. It was by the by the blood of Jesus that we received authority and power to be fruitful, to multiply and to replenish the earth and subdue it.

God wanted man to have dominion over every fish in the river, every flying fowl and over every beast of the forest. Despite what was given to Adam and Eve, they were kicked out of the Garden of Eden because of sin and this legal right to be in charge was lost; the earth was handed unto Satan (See Luke 4:6).

Nevertheless, because God so loved the world, He gave us Jesus to be the Lamb of God that took away the sins of the world.

Everyone wants to command abundance, and be fruitful and multiply, but no one wants to do what it takes to obtain this great promise. To command exceeding abundance you must be determined to learn what it takes and do what it takes to command it in your life. One great preacher said "confession without possession will lead to frustration." Once you can confess it, then you must understand and learn the know-how so that you can possess

Commanding Abundance

it. Prayer and fasting alone cannot make you command your abundance. You can have spiritual authority and jurisdiction, and not command abundance. In this race of life, there are different times and seasons. When I was a child I reasoned like a child, when I became a boy I also reasoned like a boy; as a man, I reasoned like a man.

The wisdom of God demands that everyone interested in commanding abundance in their life follow the proper instructions and necessary steps, with discipline and commitment. A great man once said, "Just any dummy will have success if he or she cares to learn and know the required ladder in life to succeed." This great man also said "you cannot climb the ladder of success dressed in the costume of failure." The man then concluded by saying, "you are born to win, but for you to win, you must prepare to win, plan to win and expect to win."

Today, I would like you to understand that in order for you to command abundance, you must **prepare** to command abundance, **plan** to command abundance, and **expect** to receive abundance in life.

CHAPTER 4

ABUNDANCE ABOVE MEASURES

Ephesians 3:20

unto him who is able to do exceedingly abundantly above all that we think and ask.

The fact that you are alive and well is abundance above measure. You know your house rent and mortgage, but if you were to pay for the natural oxygen, that you breathe in and out, it is priceless and free. That is what I means by abundance above measure.

There are millions of reason for you to celebrate abundance above measure. The bible says the gift of God is without repentance.

The ability for you to experience abundance above measure is in the power of your own hand. You are absolutely responsible for the outcome of your life. The ability to command abundance is a privilege given to us by God (Deuteronomy 30:19). God has ordained us to richly enjoy all the abundance of the earth, but Satan has vowed to steal, kill and destroy this goodly heritage. The Bible says, "Now I commend you to God and to the word of His grace which is able to build you up and give you an inheritance among them that are sanctified"

In (1 Kings 3:13). God promised to give King Solomon that which he had not asked for.

The psalmist said he shall give us the desires of our heart. Abundance above measure in my own definition means total restoration.

Commanding Abundance

Again, the American Heritage College dictionary defines the word restoration as follows: To bring back into existence or use; reestablish; to bring back to an original condition; to put someone back in a former position; to make restitution of; give back. Although man fell from the original plan of God, it has always been God's intention and will to restore everlasting life unto man! No man nor woman can create any life. I say this boldly: forget about the doctor's report, reject the proposal of the scientist about cloning, life support machines and all the new discoveries and theories. No man can create and give life; Life can only be created and given by the Almighty God. Paul said to Timothy in 1 Timothy 6:20, "O Timothy, keep that which is committed to thy trust, avoiding profane and vain babblings, and oppositions of science falsely so called." Although new facts, theories and data's are very persuading that, even the very elect are tempting to believe in it. I write to strengthen you that your faith faileth not. Isaiah 53:1 says, "Who hath believed our report? and to whom is the arm of the LORD revealed."

God has the supernatural power to do as He pleases. 1 Samuel 2:6 says, "The LORD killeth, and maketh alive: he bringeth down to the grave, and bringeth up. The LORD maketh poor, and maketh rich: he bringeth low, and lifteth up." Psalms 115:3 goes on to say, "But our God is in the heavens: he hath done whatsoever he hath pleased." This is my answer to all the new finding and new age science and technology. How will God restore life again?

Commanding Abundance

You must be born again: This is very simple; you must surrender your life to Jesus Christ. Allow Jesus to come into your life today. Make Him your Lord and Master. The bible says, in John 3:3-7, that "Jesus answered and said unto him, Verily, verily, I say unto thee, except a man be born again, he cannot see the kingdom of God. Nicodemus saith unto him, How can a man be born when he is old? can he enter the second time into his mother's womb, and be born? Jesus answered, Verily, verily, I say unto thee, except a man be born of water and of the Spirit, he cannot enter into the kingdom of God. That which is born of the flesh is flesh; and that which is born of the Spirit is spirit. Marvel not that I said unto thee, ye must be born again." This is your ultimate life insurance and Grande' assurance for life everlasting. Not only will you be

Franklin N Abazie

restored life here, you will be guaranteed and enjoy everlasting life.

CHAPTER 5

HEALING RESTORATION

Healing is children's bread.

Restoration of Health

Jeremiah 30:17

"For I will restore health unto thee, and I will heal thee of thy wounds, saith the LORD;"

Even from the days of your grandfather, sickness has always been a device of the devil. It is not the will of God for you to be sick.

2 Peter 3:9

"Not willing that any should perish but that

all should come to repentance."

It is God's will for you to be healthy all the days of your life. Jesus paid the ultimate price concerning our health on the cross (See John 19:30). Mathew 8:17 says He took away our infirmities. If He took it away, nailing it on the cross, and you believe it, then you are free from sickness and disease.

Restoration of Material Abundance

Matthew 6:33

"But seek ye first the kingdom of God, and his righteousness; and all these things shall be added unto you."

The pre-requisite to command material abundance is seeking first the kingdom of God and His righteousness; then all the material abundance will come into your life as an addition (See Matthew 6:33). Everything you desire, if you believe God and pray sincerely, will be given to you. Therefore, repent and join a bible believing church, if you do not have one. Begin to seek the kingdom of God and His righteousness and all the material abundance will be running after your life. When Job located the Lord in prayer, he received all the material abundance.

Job 42:10 "And the LORD turned the captivity of Job, when he prayed for his friends: also the LORD gave Job twice as much as he had before."

It is your turn now to turn to the Lord in prayer, go after the kingdom of God and His righteousness and watch God send all your material need. Amen.

Franklin N Abazie

Psalms 144

Blessed be the LORD, my strength, which teacheth my hands to war, and my fingers to fight: My goodness, and my fortress; my high tower, and my deliverer; my shield, and he in whom I trust; who subdueth my people under me. LORD, what is man, that thou takest knowledge of him! or the son of man, that thou makest account of him! Man is like to vanity: his days are as a shadow that passeth away. Bow thy heavens, O LORD, and come down: touch the mountains, and they shall smoke. Cast forth lightning, and scatter them: shoot out thine arrows, and destroy them. Send thine hand from above; rid me, and deliver me out of great waters, from the hand of strange children; Whose mouth speaketh vanity, and their right hand is a right hand of falsehood. I will sing a new song unto thee,

Commanding Abundance

O God: upon a psaltery and an instrument of ten strings will I sing praises unto thee. It is he that giveth salvation unto kings: who delivereth David his servant from the hurtful sword. Rid me, and deliver me from the hand of strange children, whose mouth speaketh vanity, and their right hand is a right hand of falsehood: That our sons may be as plants grown up in their youth; that our daughters may be as corner stones, polished after the similitude of a palace: That our garners may be full, affording all manner of store: that our sheep may bring forth thousands and ten thousands in our streets: That our oxen may be strong to labour; that there be no breaking in, nor going out; that there be no complaining in our streets. Happy is that people, that is in such a case: yea, happy is that people, whose God is the LORD.

CHAPTER 6

PRAYER POINTS FOR ABUNDANCE

Now read Psalms 35:18-27, Psalms 51:1-11, Job 42:10-12.

Begin to pray:

1. O Lord of abundance, visit me with a change, in the name of Jesus.

2. Merciful Father of grace, locate me with a solution, in the name of Jesus.

3. Omnipotent Father of grace, grant me divine speed, in the name of Jesus.

4. Possessor of heaven, place your mantle of power on me, in the name of Jesus.

5. Fire of God, break every hindrance against me, in the name of Jesus.

6. Power of God, locate me.

7. Fire of God, burn every hindering power, in the name of Jesus.

8. Father Lord, grant me my own abundance.

9. Almighty Father, permit me to possess my abundance, in the name of Jesus.

10. Finger of God, bring me out of the pit of poverty, in the name of Jesus.

Congratulation, your prayers have been answered. Amen

Commanding Abundance

The pre-requisite steps to command abundance are:

1. You must Plan to succeed.

2. Be prepared to succeed

3. Expect to succeed.

I want you to know that anyone can command abundance, if he or she cares to know what it takes to command abundance. Our God is not a partial God. The bible says the wealth of the wicked shall be laid up for the just. It is therefore wise to learn the necessary steps to command abundance, focus on it, work at it and you will command your abundance. Jesus is Lord.

PRAYER OF SALVATION

Determine your Divine Visitation

Mathew 11:28 Come unto me all ye that labor and are heavy laden, and I will give you rest.

Jeremiah 29:13-14

And ye shall seek me and find me when ye shall search for me with all your heart.

I will be found of you; Saith the Lord: and I will turn away your captivityGod's visitation is what we call divine visitation. It is divine visitation that will cure all frustration. The mandate of our commission will speak into your life to restore health to you and heal you of all your wounds, only when you are set for an encounter! I want you to know the truth! The truth is that Jesus died for your sins and because He died you must be alive and prosperous.

What must I do to determine my divine visitation?

To determine divine visitation, you must be born again! The word says as many as received him, to them gave He power to become the sons of God. Even to them that believe on his name.

To qualify for divine visitation do the following with sincerity 1) Acknowledge that you are a sinner and that He died for you. Romans 3:23.

2) **Repent** of your sins. Acts 3:19, Luke 13:5, 2 Peter 3:9

3) **Believe** in your heart that Jesus died for your sins. Romans 10:10

4) **Confess** Jesus as Lord over your life. Romans 10:10, Acts 2:21

Now repeat this Prayer after me

Say Lord Jesus, I accept you today, as my Lord and my Savior; forgive me of my sins and wash me with your blood. Right now, I believe I am sanctified, saved and set free. I am free from the power of sin to serve the Lord Jesus. Thank you Lord for saving me, Amen.

Congratulations: YOU ARE NOW ABORN AGAIN CHRISTAIN

AGAIN I SAY TO YOU CONGRATULATIONS

I adjure you to watch the Spirit of God bear witness with your Spirit, confirming His word with signs that will follow. The word says that the Spirit itself beareth witness with our spirit, that we are the children of God.

Miracle Care Outreach

"…But that the members should have the same care one for another" 1 Corinthians 12:25

We are all members of the body of Christ. Jesus commanded us to love our neighbor as ourselves. This includes caring for one another as a member of one body. True love is expressed in caring and giving. The word says for God so Loved, He gave….

Reach out to someone in need, care and help them find Jesus the Healer. Invite them to our

Home Care Cell Fellowship groups (Miracle Satellite Fellowship) In the USA at 33 Schley Street Newark New Jersey 07112.You can also locate other locations near your area. Or, if you are in Nigeria, go to Miracle of God Ministries" **Miracle Chapel** Mpama – Egbu-Owerri Imo state Nigeria. Everyone is part of the family in Christ. Identify with your covenant family (Home Care Cell Fellowship Group). We meet every Tuesday at 6:00pm-7:00pm

LIFE IS NOT ABOUT DURATION BUT ABOUT DONATION

Now that you are born again, the great commission demands you should evangelize and bring someone to Jesus.

Now that you have received your healing &

miracles, it is your turn to bring someone to receive their own healing and miracles for themselves.

Extend an invitation to your friends and families.

Disciple and bring someone to church.

John 1:45

Philip findeth Nathanael....

Become a soul winner and watch God turn around your life.

It is your assignment to bring someone to be a partaker of our Healing commission.

ABOUT THE AUTHOR

Rev Franklin N Abazie is the founding and Presiding Pastor of Miracle of God Healing Church with headquarters in Newark, New Jersey USA and a branch church in Owerri-Imo State Nigeria. He is following the footsteps of one of his mentors, Oral Roberts (Healing Evangelist) of the blessed memory. The Lord passed Oral Roberts healing mantle two days before he went to be with the Lord at age 91 into the hand of healing evangelist-Rev Franklin N Abazie in a vision. In all his services the Power and Presence of God is present to heal all in his audience. He is an ordained man of God with a Healing Ministry reviving the healing and miracle ministry of Jesus Christ of Nazareth.

Franklin N Abazie

Pastor Franklin N Abazie, is called by God with a unique mandate: "THE MOMENT IS DUE TO IMPACT YOUR WORLD THROUGH THE REVIVAL OF THE HEALING & MIRACLE MINISTRY OF JESUS CHRIST OF NAZARETH

I AM SENDING YOU TO RESTORE HEALTH UNTO THEE AND I WILL HEAL THEE OF THY WOUNDS. SAID THE LORD OF HOST"

He is a gifted ardent Teacher of the word of God who operates also in the office of a Prophet, generating and attracting undeniable signs & wonders, special miracles and healings, with apostolic fireworks of the Holy Ghost. He is the founding and presiding senior Pastor of this fast growing Healing ministry. He has written over 86 inspirational, healing and transforming books covering almost all aspect of divine healing and life. He is happily married and blessed with children.

OTHER BOOKS BY THE AUTHOR BY REV FRANKLIN N ABAZIE

1) The Outcome of Faith

2) Understanding the secret of prevailing Prayers

3) Commanding Abundance

4) Understanding the secret of the man God uses

5) Activating My Due Season

6) Overcoming Divine Verdicts

7) The Outcome of Divine Wisdom

8) Understanding God's Restoration Mandate

9) Walking in Victory and Authority of the Truth

10) Understanding Gods Covenant Exemption

11) Destiny Restoration Pillars

12) Provoking Acceptable Praise

13) Understanding Divine Judgment

14) Activating Angelic Re-enforcement

15) Provoking Un-Merited Favor

16) The Benefits of the Speaking faith

17) Understanding Divine Arrangement

18) How to Keep Your Healing

19) Understanding the mysteries of the Speaking Faith

20) Understanding the Mysteries of Prophetic Healing

21) Operating under the Rules of Creative Healing

22) Understanding the joy of Breakthrough

23) Understanding the Mystery of Breakthrough.

24) Understanding Divine Prosperity

25) Understanding Divine Healing

26) Retaining Your Inheritance

27) Overcoming confusing Spirit

28) Commanding Angelic Escorts

29) Possessing Your inheritance in Christ Jesus

30) Understanding Your Guardian Angels

31) Overcoming the Dominion of Sin

32) Understanding the Voice of God

33) The Outstanding benefits of the Anointing

34) The Audacity of the Blood of Jesus

35) Walking in the Reality of the Anointing

36) Escaping the Nightmares of Poverty

37) Understanding Your Harvest Season

Commanding Abundance

38) Activating Your Success Buttons

39) Overcoming the forces of Darkness

40) Overcoming the devices of the Devil

41) Overcoming Demonic agents

42) Overcoming the sorrows of failure

43) Restoration of broken Marriages

44) Redeeming Your Days

45) The force of Vision

46) Overcoming the forces of ignorance

47) Understanding Divine Arrangement

48) Understanding the sacrifice of small beginning

49) The Principles and Power of small beginning

50) Understanding the mystery of Prophesy

51) Overcoming Dream nightmares

52) Breaking the shackles of the curse of the law

53) Understanding the Joy of harvest

54) Wisdom for Signs & Wonders

55) Wisdom for generational Impact

56) Wisdom for Marriage Stability

57) Understanding the number of your Days

58) Enforcing Your Kingdom Rights

59) Escaping the traps of immoralities

Commanding Abundance

60) Escaping the trap of Poverty

61) Accessing Biblical Prosperity

62) Accessing True Riches in Christ

63) Silencing the Voice of the Accuser

64) Overcoming the forces of oppositions

65) Quenching the voice of the avenger

66) Silencing Oppositions & Contemporaries

67) Silencing Your Mockers

68) Understanding the Power of the Holy Ghost

69) Understanding the Baptism of Power

70) The Mystery of the Blood of Jesus

71) Understanding the Mystery of Sanctification

72) Understanding the Power of Holiness

73) Understanding the forces of Purity

74) Activating the Forces of Vengeance

75) The Mystery of Restoration

76) Overcoming Demonic Prediction 77) Engaging the mystery of the blood

78) Commanding the Power of the Speaking faith

79) Uprooting the forces against Your Rising

80) Overcoming mere success syndrome

81) Understanding Divine Sentence

82) Understanding the Mystery of Praise

83) Understanding the Author of Faith

84) The Mystery of the finisher of faith

MY HEART FELT SINCERE PRAYER FOR YOU

It is my desire that you meet God through one of our teachings or books. It is my sincere prayer that, after you have gone through this book, you encounter God through His word. It was not by accident that you have this book in your hands. Therefore, permit me to pray over your life now.

Heavenly Father, I pray that you touch this precious soul and grant them an encounter that will transform their life, in the mighty name of Jesus. Lord touch them and release unto them the Spirit to command abundance, in the mighty name of Jesus.

Commanding Abundance

www.ingramcontent.com/pod-product-compliance
Lightning Source LLC
Chambersburg PA
CBHW040325300426
44112CB00021B/2884